Contents

Introduction	2
1. The Age of Explorers	4
2. Smooth Sailing	10
3. Choppy Waters	14
4. Disaster	20
5. Rescue	26
6. Search for the Lost Ship	34
7. Discovering *Endurance*	38
Glossary	46
Index	47

Introduction

Three thousand metres beneath the Weddell Sea lies the ghost of a great ship. Long ago, *Endurance* set sail on a quest to explore the South Pole. The mission was abandoned when the ship became trapped in sea ice less than 100 miles off the coast of Antarctica.

The crew never reached the South Pole. They escaped the sinking ship and began an epic polar adventure. It was really hard, but they all survived. Expedition leader Ernest Shackleton was praised for his courage.

But *Endurance* was never seen again ...

Fact

Endurance is the ability to keep going when the going gets tough.

Until now.

Scientists have discovered the location of *Endurance* deep below the freezing waves. The sunken ship is a home for animals like sea squirts, anemones, sponges and starfish. But why did Shackleton set sail for Antarctica in the first place? Why did *Endurance* sink, and how did the crew escape? What led to the ship's discovery over 100 years later?

We are going on a journey to investigate these questions. Have *you* got the endurance to survive?

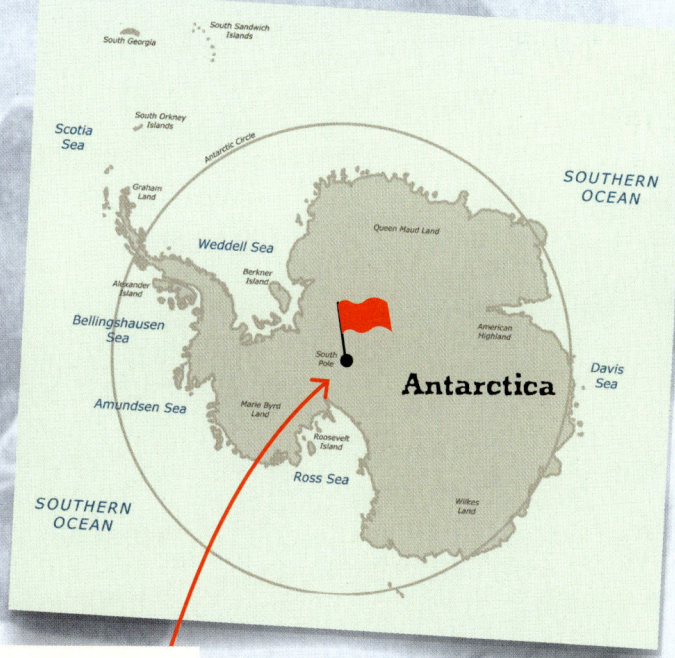

The South Pole is the most southern point in the world.

1 The Age of Explorers

Our story began in London in 1913, where Shackleton was raising money for his expedition to the South Pole. It wasn't his first trip to Antarctica – Shackleton was a crew member on Captain Scott's famous ship, *Discovery*, in 1901. He had also led his own mission on a ship called *Nimrod* in 1907.

Discovery and *Nimrod* tried to reach the South Pole — something that no human had ever done. But terrible weather and sickness forced the crews of both missions to turn back.

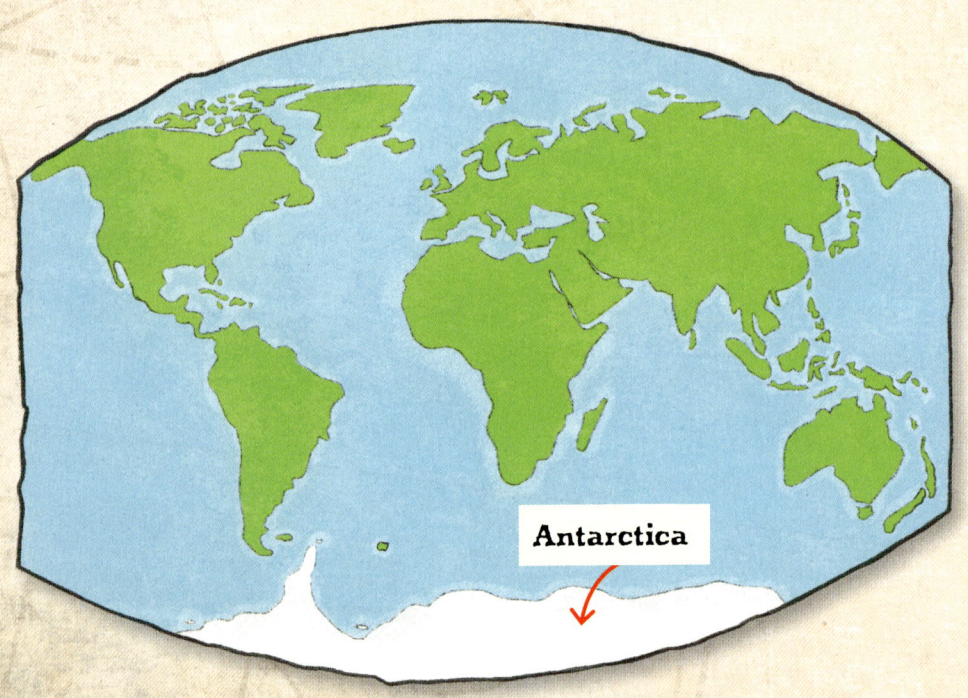

↑ The continent of Antarctica is the coldest place on Earth!

Race to the South Pole

British explorer Captain Scott and Norwegian explorer Roald Amundsen both wanted to be the first to reach the South Pole. It had become a race! Scott set off again in 1910 on a ship called *Terra Nova*, but Amundsen beat him there on 14th December 1911. Scott reached the pole 33 days later, but sadly died on the expedition.

Shackleton wanted to cross Antarctica from the Weddell Sea to the Ross Sea. Not even Amundsen had managed to do that!

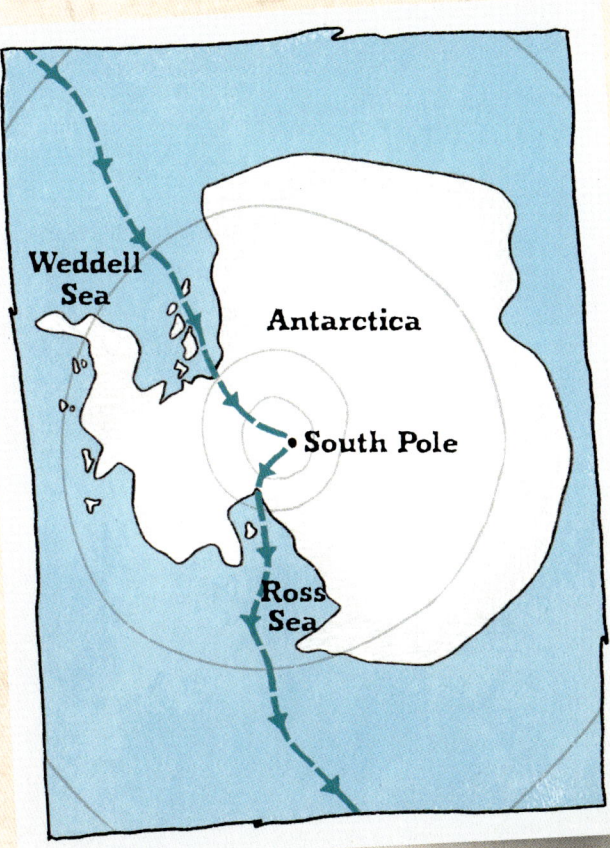

I felt strangely drawn to the mysterious south.

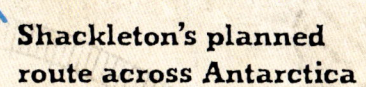

↑ Shackleton's planned route across Antarctica

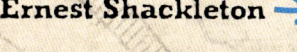

Ernest Shackleton →

Shackleton was born in Ireland in 1874 and moved to England as a boy. He had always dreamed of adventure. But it took more than dreams to launch an expedition to Antarctica. He would have to find a strong ship and a team of fearless sailors. And for this, he needed money!

Luckily for Shackleton, his wife Emily came from a wealthy family. She knew rich and important people.

Don't worry, Ernest. I have friends who can help.

← Emily Shackleton

Emily's friend Janet Stancomb-Wills had plenty of money. She liked to use it for good causes, like supporting the fire brigade and helping artists. She thought it was important to learn more about Antarctica, and she agreed to give Shackleton money for his expedition.

I believe it is important to learn more about the frozen south.

↑ Janet Stancomb-Wills

With Emily's help, Shackleton managed to get the money together to buy his dream ship. He named it *Endurance* after the Shackleton family motto:

By Endurance, We Conquer

At first, *Endurance* was called *Polaris*. It was supposed to take tourists to the North Pole. The ship's owners ran into money problems and agreed to sell it for less than it was worth. So Shackleton bought *Polaris* and renamed it *Endurance* for his expedition to the South Pole.

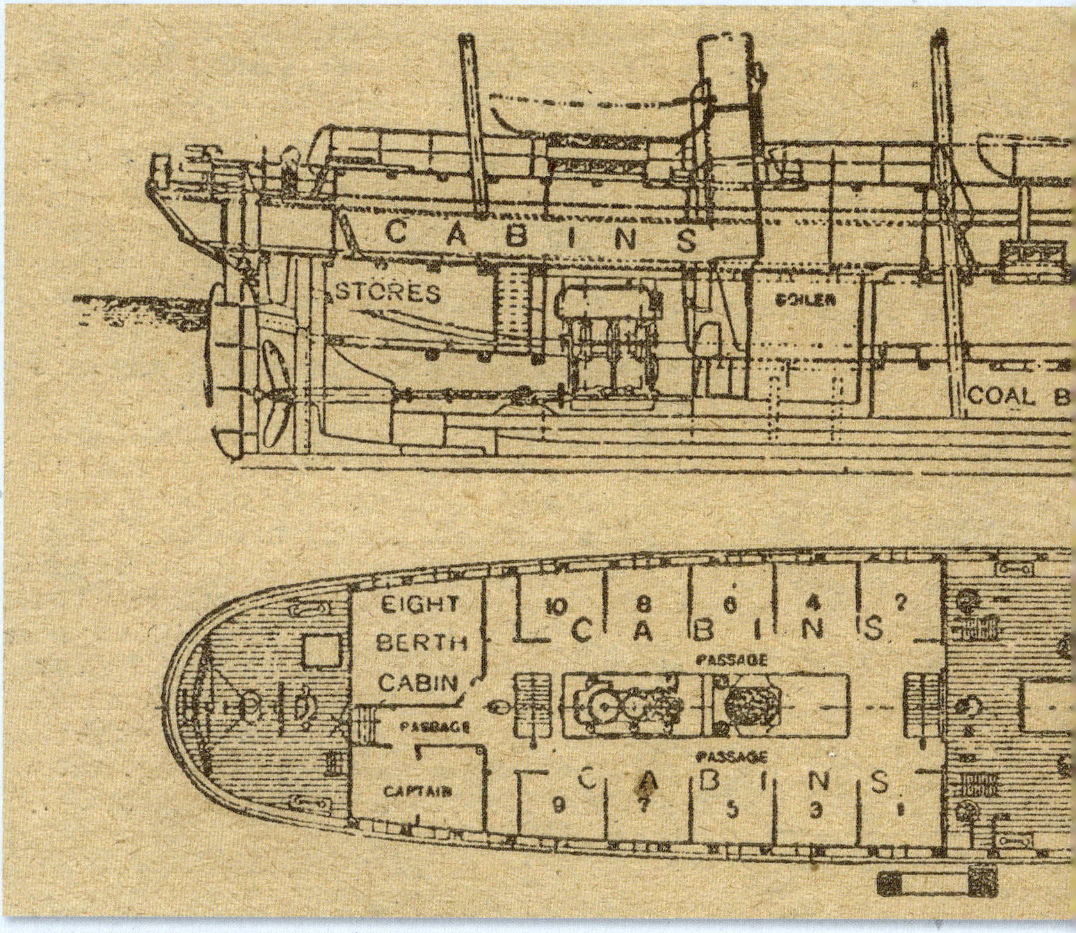

Fact

Endurance was one of the strongest ships in the world. It was built to cope with thick ice.

But before *Endurance* could start its voyage, it needed a crew.

News got around about the expedition, and a lot of people wanted to join the trip. In those days, women were expected to stay at home. Only men were allowed to apply, and thousands of them did. In the end, Shackleton chose almost 30 men to join him.

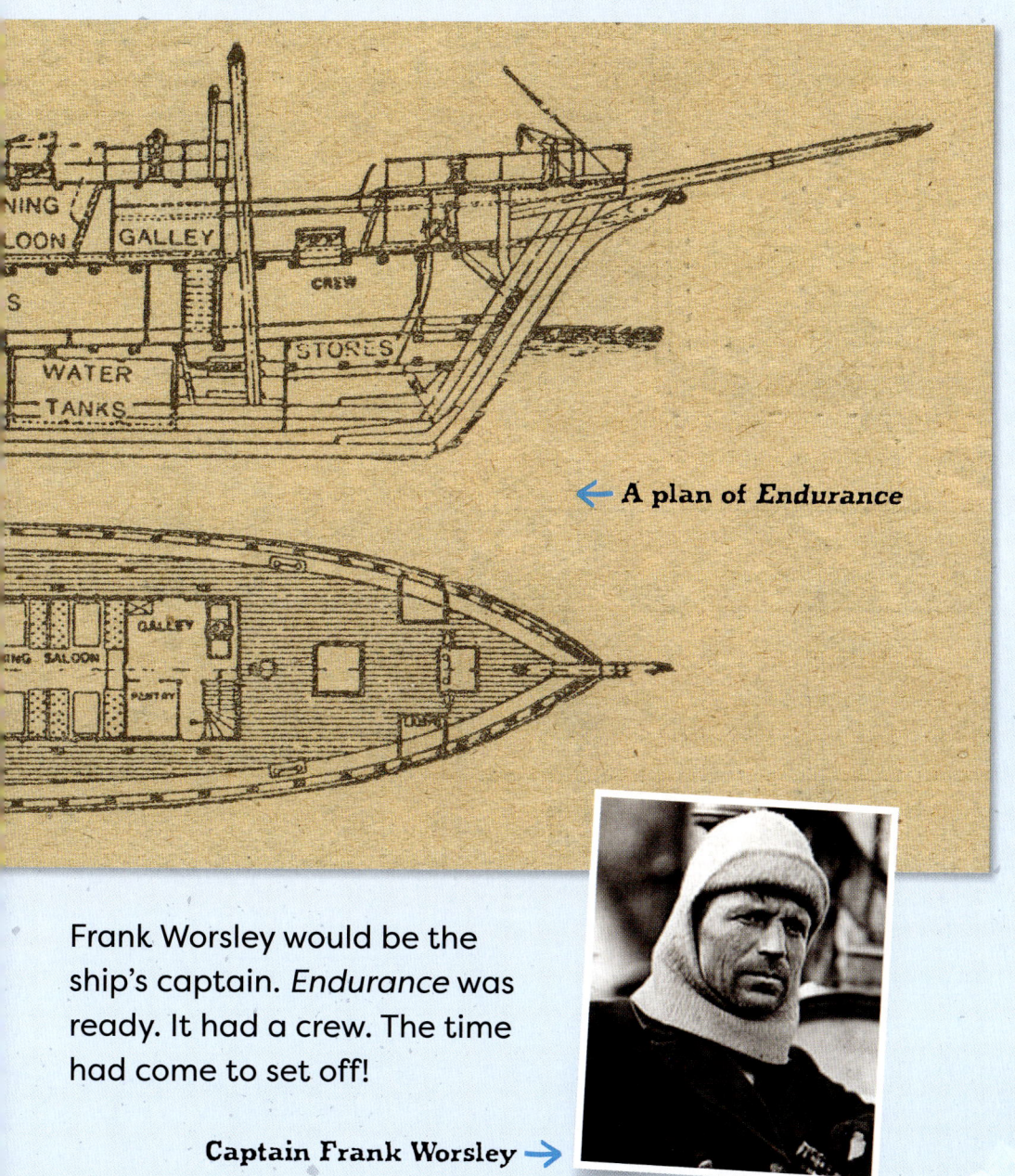

← A plan of *Endurance*

Frank Worsley would be the ship's captain. *Endurance* was ready. It had a crew. The time had come to set off!

Captain Frank Worsley →

2 Smooth Sailing

Endurance set sail on Saturday 8th August 1914.

Endurance – expedition plan

Mission: To be the first humans to cross Antarctica from 'sea to sea'. The plan was that *Endurance* would reach Antarctica on the shores of the Weddell Sea. From there, a team would cross the frozen **continent** by land using sledge dogs. They would pass through the South Pole on their way to the Ross Sea, where they would be met by a second team. This second team would gather lots of scientific information and would help the rest of the crew to return home on a different ship.

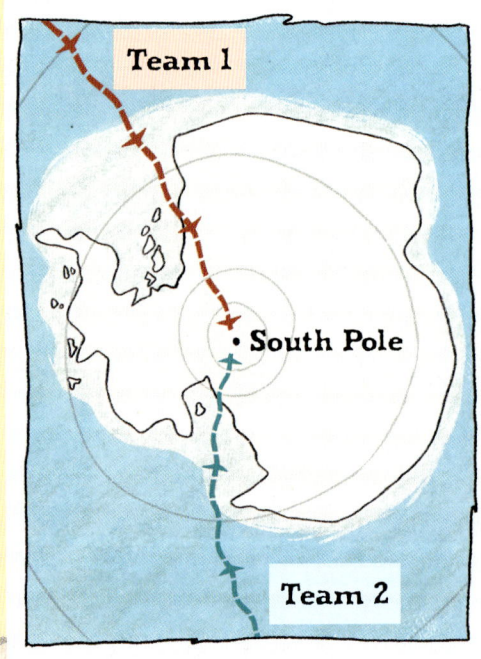

10

The dogs

Sixty-nine dogs were chosen to join *Endurance*. Shackleton planned to use sledges to drag food and supplies across the ice; he knew from his earlier trips to Antarctica that dogs were better than humans at pulling sledges.

↑ Colonel

↑ Sledge dog in harness

↑ Basilisk and Ginger

↑ Tom Crean, a member of the *Endurance* crew, with sledge dog puppies

The long journey from Europe to South America went smoothly, although two members of the crew were sent home for misbehaving. One of them was replaced by a Canadian sailor with lots of experience. The other was replaced by a young Welsh **stowaway** called Perce Blackborow.

Stowaway

Perce Blackborow was only 19 years old when he secretly boarded *Endurance* in search of adventure.

Sir Ernest, I've always wanted to see the world. If you let me stay, I'll work harder than anyone!

Shackleton allowed the daring stowaway to stay. The final member of the crew was a tabby cat, Mrs Chippy. The ship travelled south to the faraway South Georgia Island in the Atlantic Ocean.

↑ Perce Blackborow

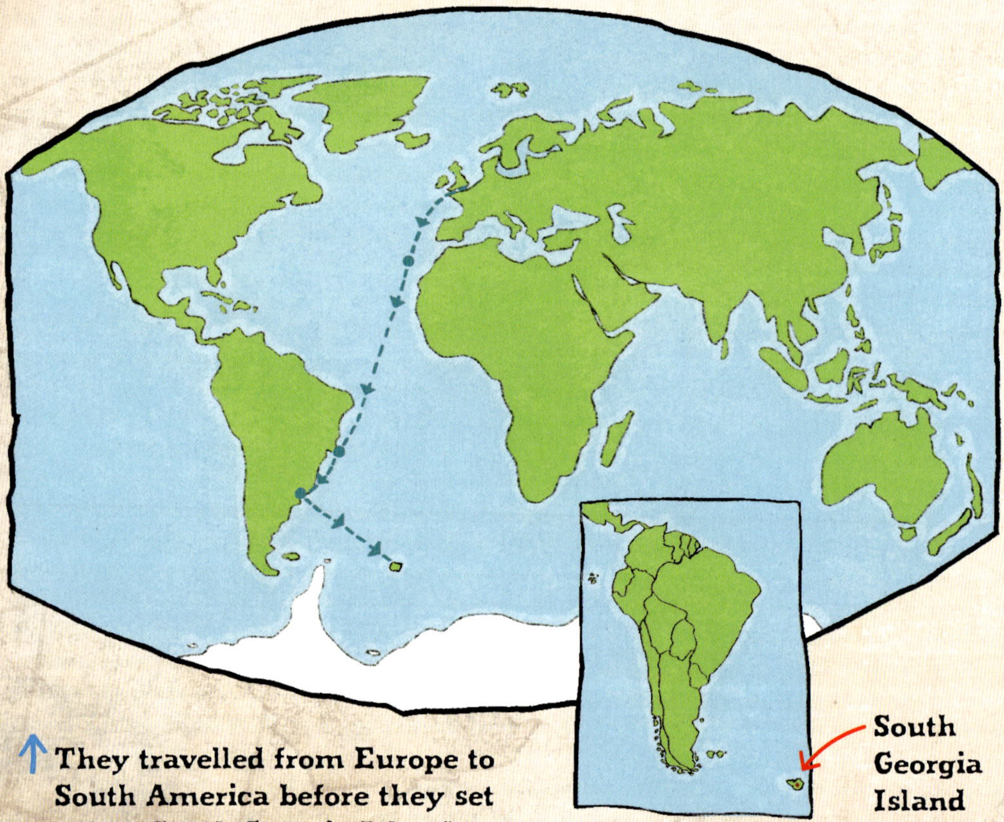

↑ They travelled from Europe to South America before they set off for South Georgia Island.

South Georgia Island

The crew spent time on South Georgia Island loading the ship with food and other things they would need for the rest of the journey. About four months after it set sail from England, *Endurance* was finally ready for the most dangerous part of its mission: through the freezing waters of Antarctica.

↑ Perce Blackborow and Mrs Chippy

Mrs Chippy

The ship's cat was called Mrs Chippy because he was often to be found with the 'chippy' or **carpenter**. Yes, you read that right – Mrs Chippy was a boy! By the time the crew realised this fact, the name had already stuck.

3 Choppy Waters

Endurance sailed towards the Weddell Sea as the mountains of South Georgia Island faded into mist. Danger loomed from the grey swirling waves. Giant icebergs bobbed up around the ship, but it kept going. On 7th December 1914 – only two days after leaving South Georgia Island – *Endurance* reached the pack ice.

Pack ice

Pack ice is made up of large chunks of ice that drift on the surface of the sea. From far above, it looks like a giant white jigsaw puzzle.

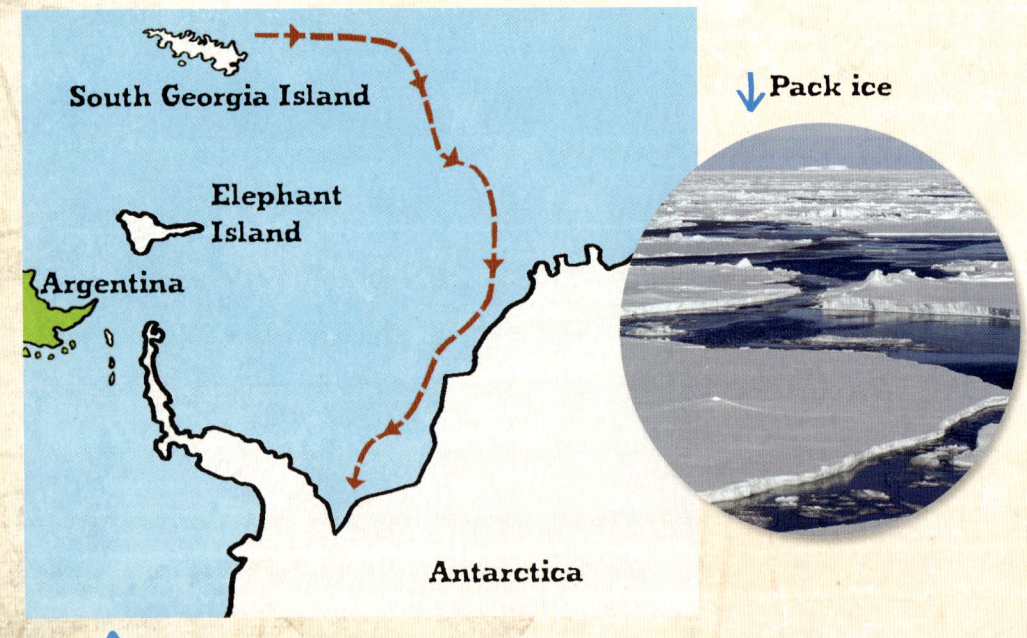

↑ They travelled from South Georgia Island to the Weddell Sea.

Iceberg

An iceberg is a huge lump of ice that floats in the seas around the North Pole and South Pole. Some icebergs can be several kilometres wide, but only a small part called the 'berg' is visible above water.

TRUE or FALSE?

True or false? Unlike the sea, icebergs are formed from fresh water, not salty water. See below to find out.

↓ Iceberg

We drifted past some magnificent icebergs.

↑ Frank Hurley, ship's photographer

True! Icebergs are chunks of **glaciers** or **ice shelves** that have broken away from land. The frozen water in an iceberg is fresh, not salty.

Endurance did its best to **navigate** these massive lumps of ice. The Weddell Sea, north of Antarctica, is known for being particularly dangerous. The seawater moves around the continent in a **clockwise** motion. It drags icebergs and pack ice along with it, tugging them towards passing ships. Shackleton knew that they had to be very careful.

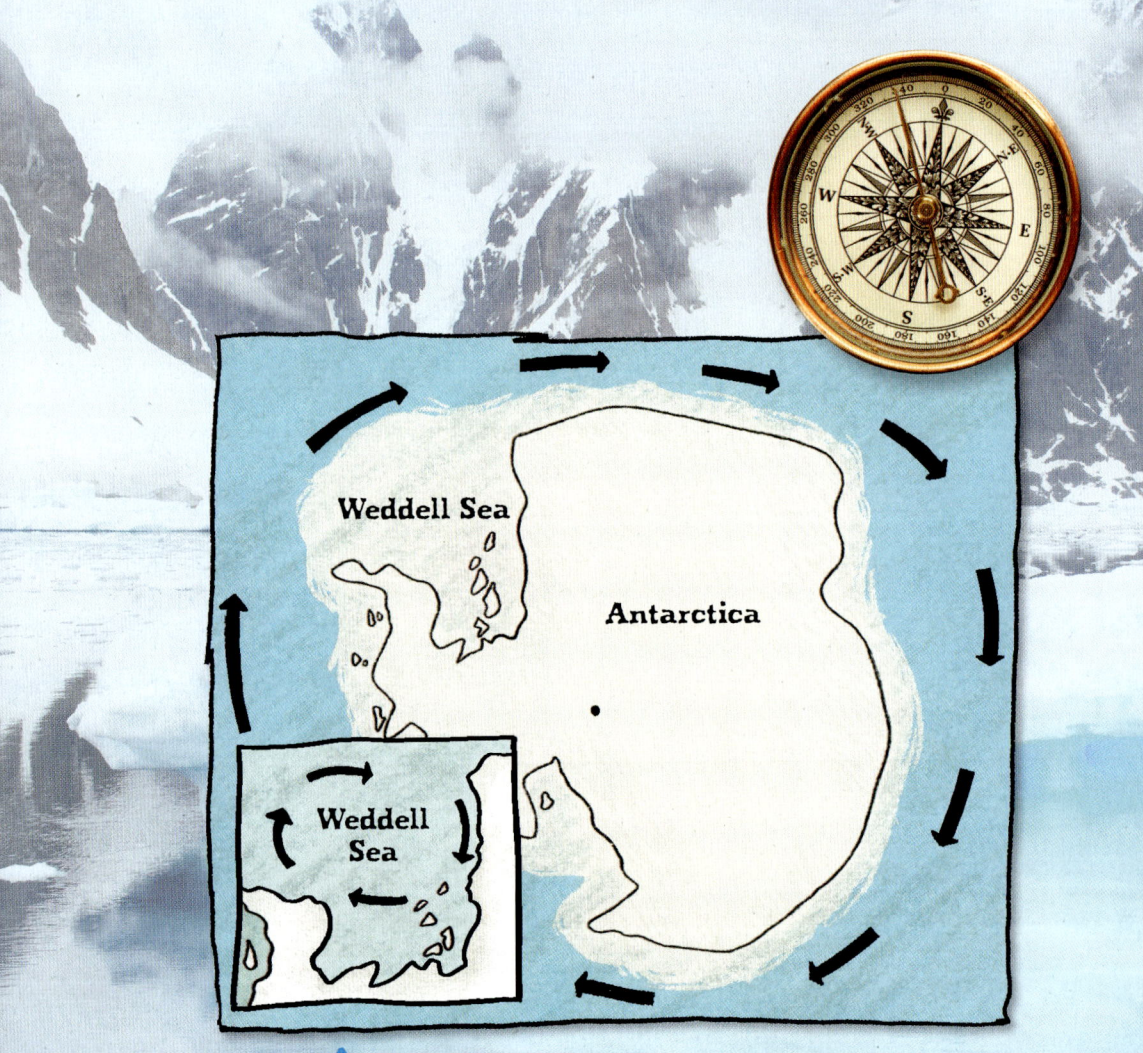

↑ Seawater moves around Antarctica in a clockwise direction.

About a month after leaving South Georgia Island, the crew caught sight of the north-west coast of Antarctica. Land was still far away, but at least they could see it! The ship broke free from the pack ice into open water, making for a bay where it could **dock**. But the pack ice slowly crept closer again.

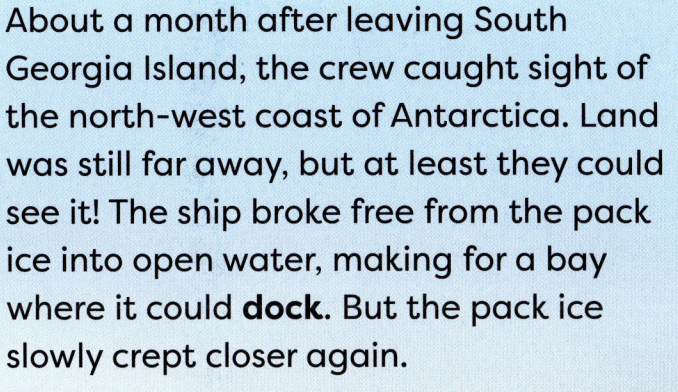

Breakfast

A lot of people say that breakfast is the most important meal of the day. Crew members on *Endurance* ate a hearty breakfast of things like oats and seal's liver.

The pack ice closed around the ship. *Endurance* had to ram the ice to break through and move closer to land. The pack ice became thicker and tougher. On 22nd February 1915, only one hundred kilometres from land, the ship stopped completely. The weather was bad, the air freezing cold. The ship nudged the ice, but it couldn't get through.

Endurance was stuck.

↓ ***Endurance* trapped in the pack ice**

The ship would not be able to move until the ice had shifted. Over the long, dark days of winter, the men exercised the dogs on the solid pack ice, leading them in sledge races. On Midwinter's Day, 21st June 1915, the crew celebrated with speeches and songs.

As the sun began to return to the frozen land, everyone felt happier. Surely the ice would break up now the sun had returned. Eventually, *Endurance* started to move forward again. Shackleton and the crew were hopeful that the ship would finally reach the shores of Antarctica.

Sadly, they were wrong.

Dark days

Antarctica is at the south of the Earth. When it's summer in northern countries like the UK, it's winter in Antarctica. During Antarctic winters, Antarctica is the furthest point from the sun, so it is dark in the daytime as well as at night.

4 Disaster

A storm raged over the Weddell Sea. The ice closed in again, pinning *Endurance* in place and, weighing the ship down. The wood began to crack. Henry McNeish, the carpenter, did his best to patch up holes, but there was nothing that could be done. Shackleton ordered the crew to get off *Endurance* for the final time. They stood on solid ice, watching as the ship began to tip sideways.

↓ Captain Frank Worsley

*Our ship has been magnificent ... It will be sad if such a brave little **craft** should be finally crushed by the Weddell pack ice.*

On 21st November 1915, *Endurance* finally sank beneath the waves.

Almost a year after leaving South Georgia Island, the crew found themselves stuck on the pack ice. They had saved the three lifeboats before *Endurance* sank, together with food and other supplies. At first, Shackleton led his crew towards Antarctica, but the ice was drifting back towards the sea. Once the drifting ice reached open water, the crew would use the lifeboats to escape to a nearby island.

The mission had changed. Shackleton was no longer trying to cross Antarctica: he was trying to save his crew.

2. Once the crew reached open water, they would use the lifeboats.

Pack ice

1. First the crew would escape in sleds over the ice.

Land

After months camping on the pack ice, Shackleton was worried: they were starting to run out of food and the ice beneath them was breaking up. If they stayed any longer, they might drown! The crew climbed into the three lifeboats. They would have to make it through chunks of ice if they wanted to reach solid land.

⬆ Today, one of the crew's three lifeboats is on display at the school Shackleton attended in London.

They headed for a distant group of islands with only a compass to guide them. The journey was very difficult. The tired men rowed through the choppy waters as black-and-white **orcas** swam loops around them.

Orcas →

After days of non-stop rowing, the men were exhausted. They urgently needed to reach land so that they could rest. The closest place was the remote Elephant Island. Grey mists swirled around the island. Water bashed the jagged rocks. Reaching it was not going to be easy. The crew fought for hours against the waves, hardly moving any closer. At last, all three lifeboats landed on a stony beach beneath the dangerous cliffs of Elephant Island. They were finally on solid ground.

I doubted if all the men would survive that night.

← Ernest Shackleton

The crew were suffering from thirst, extreme tiredness and **frostbite**. Elephant Island was battered by wind. There were no other humans there, and the food from the lifeboats wouldn't last forever. What were they going to do?

They needed a ship to get them home to England. Shackleton knew that there was a **whaling station** on South Georgia Island – he had visited it on the way to Antarctica. The men at the station could help them.

If his crew were going to survive, Shackleton would have to make another dangerous journey.

5 Rescue

Shackleton left for South Georgia Island on the largest lifeboat, the *James Caird*, along with Henry McNeish, Captain Frank Worsley and three other men. The rest of the crew cheered as the boat set off, hopeful that Shackleton would find help and that they would be saved.

For ten days, Shackleton and his five crewmates battled the wild sea. Waves lashed the boat, spilling over the deck. McNeish worked hard to fix any leaks.

The going was tough. Sea birds screeched overhead. Penguins shuffled past on drifts of ice.

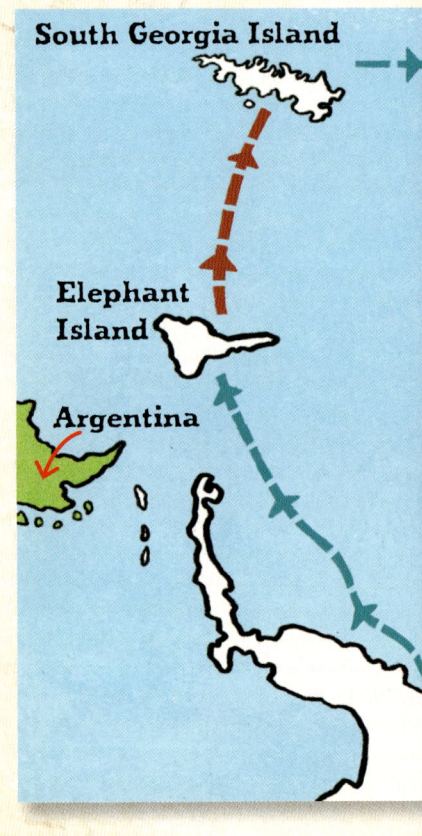

The weather out here is awful.

TRUE or FALSE?

True or false? Polar bears live in Antarctica. See the next page to find out.

← Henry McNeish, ship's carpenter

The *James Caird* arrived on the shores of South Georgia Island, almost 1300 kilometres from Elephant Island. But their mission was far from over …

↑ The red line shows the route Shackleton took from Elephant Island to South Georgia Island. The blue line shows the expedition's earlier journey.

The coast was deserted. Shackleton needed to reach the whaling station on the other side of South Georgia Island. It would be quickest to cross by land, but would that even be possible? The island was full of glaciers and jagged peaks covered in ice. Shackleton decided to take the risk.

False! Polar bears live near the North Pole.

Shackleton split up the small group. Three men would stay behind with the lifeboat. He and two others, including Captain Worsley, would hike across South Georgia Island to the whaling station to find help.

South Georgia Island

South Georgia Island is an important stop for Antarctic expeditions. It has been a base for whaling and hunting for over 200 years, but there are no human towns or villages on the island. It is thought that explorer Captain James Cook was the first person to set foot on South Georgia Island, in 1775.

↑ South Georgia Island

Shackleton before the expedition ...

... and after many months in Antarctica

After over 36 hours of hiking in terrible winds, the men could see the whaling station far below them. The station lay at the bottom of a hill. An icy stream tumbled down the hillside. It would take hours to follow another route, and the men were hungry and desperate for rest. They decided to slide down the stream to the station. They arrived soaking wet and shivering with cold, in clothes that hadn't been washed in months. Their hair was long and their faces were unshaven. The manager of the whaling station had met Shackleton when *Endurance* first arrived on South Georgia Island many months before – but he didn't recognise him!

↑ Boats and men awaiting rescue on Elephant Island

Shackleton and his two crewmates were safe at the whaling station. They enjoyed hot baths and good meals, and could finally sleep. But what about the rest of the team?

Captain Worsley borrowed a ship from the whaling station to rescue the three men who were waiting on the other side of South Georgia Island. They were sheltering under the upturned lifeboat. The ship couldn't sail back with them straight away because of a storm at sea, but at last they arrived safely at the whaling station.

Fact

Elephant Island takes its name from its shape, which is similar to an elephant's head. It was also where elephant seals were seen by Captain George Powell in 1821 – one of their earliest sightings.

Journeys back to England were arranged for McNeish and two of the others. Shackleton stayed to rescue his remaining 22 crewmates, who were waiting on Elephant Island. Time was running out for them, alone, without much food or shelter, in one of the coldest places on Earth.

Shackleton tried to reach the men with three different ships, but none of them were **ice-breakers**, and they couldn't get beyond the giant sheets of ice that had closed in around Elephant Island. Each ship was forced to turn back.

↑ The remaining crew on Elephant Island

↓ Shackleton returned to Elephant Island to rescue the rest of the crew.

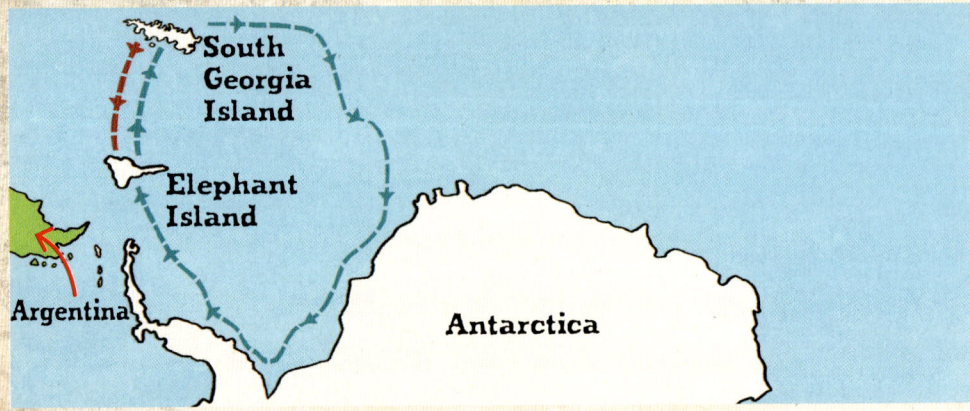

The failed attempts to rescue the crew were difficult for Shackleton. He was frustrated by the delays and worried that the men would starve or freeze to death.

Shackleton finally found a ship that could reach the shores of Elephant Island. Incredibly, all 22 men were alive. They had survived the terrible cold by camping beneath the two remaining lifeboats.

It was time to come home. Twenty-four months and 22 days since leaving England, every single member of the *Endurance* crew was safe!

↑ Shackleton's rescue of the men on Elephant Island

My Darling,

I have done it ... Not a life lost and we have been through hell.

← **Letter from Ernest to Emily Shackleton**

Shackleton returned to Britain a hero. There were even stamps and postcards made to commemorate his journey. →

6 Search for the Lost Ship

Shackleton's journey has become a legend. In the end, he was unable to cross Antarctica from sea to sea. So, in a way, his mission was a failure. But Shackleton's success at leading almost 30 men through near-impossible challenges means he is remembered as a hero.

No matter how bad things got, he never gave up! Isn't that what endurance is all about?

Over the years, many people have wanted to find the place where *Endurance* sank in the Weddell Sea. Until 2022, no one ever had.

The Weddell Sea

Reaching down from the Southern Ocean, the Weddell Sea is absolutely huge. It covers over one-and-a-half million square kilometres! It is home to many thousands of **species** of animals, including seals, whales and penguins.

As well as the Weddell Sea's vast size and faraway location, the greatest challenge to finding the ship was the pack ice. As we have discovered, giant chunks of ice cover the Weddell Sea in a complex jigsaw puzzle.

The movement of the ice can change quickly. The tough conditions make such journeys expensive and full of danger, even today.

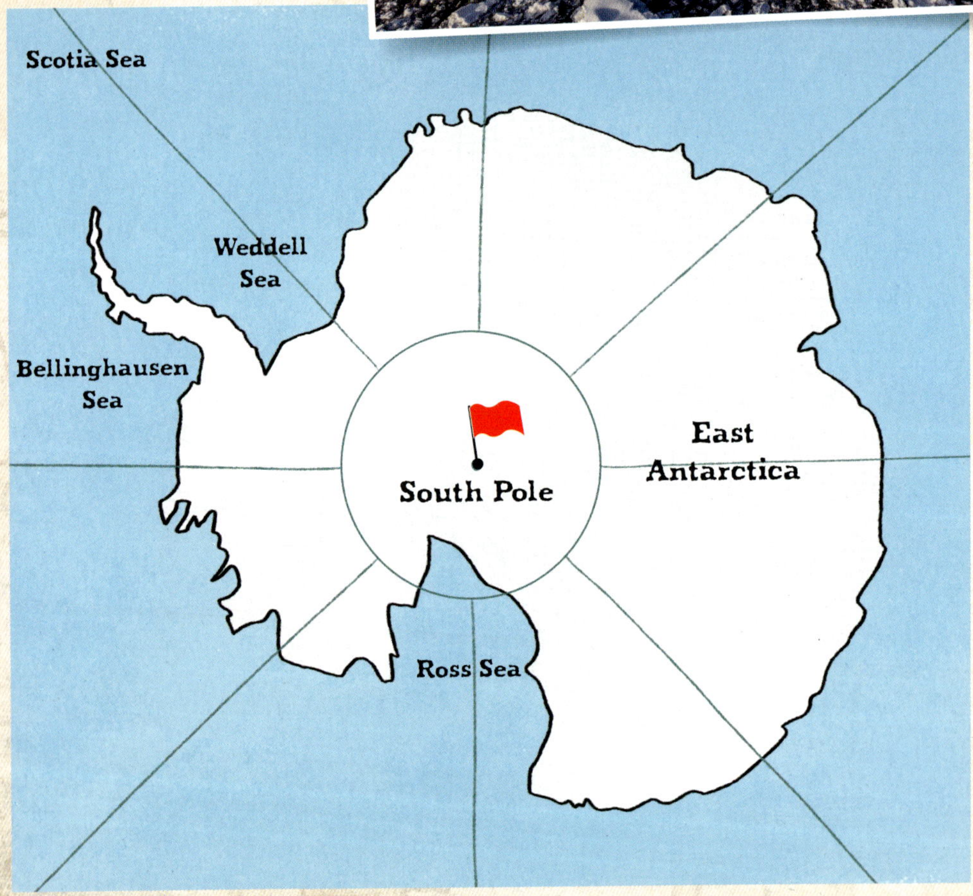

⬆ This map shows the main seas around Antarctica.

36

PENGUIN FACT FILE

Penguins are among the amazing animals that have learned to live in this extreme climate.

Emperor penguins are the largest species of penguin on Earth.

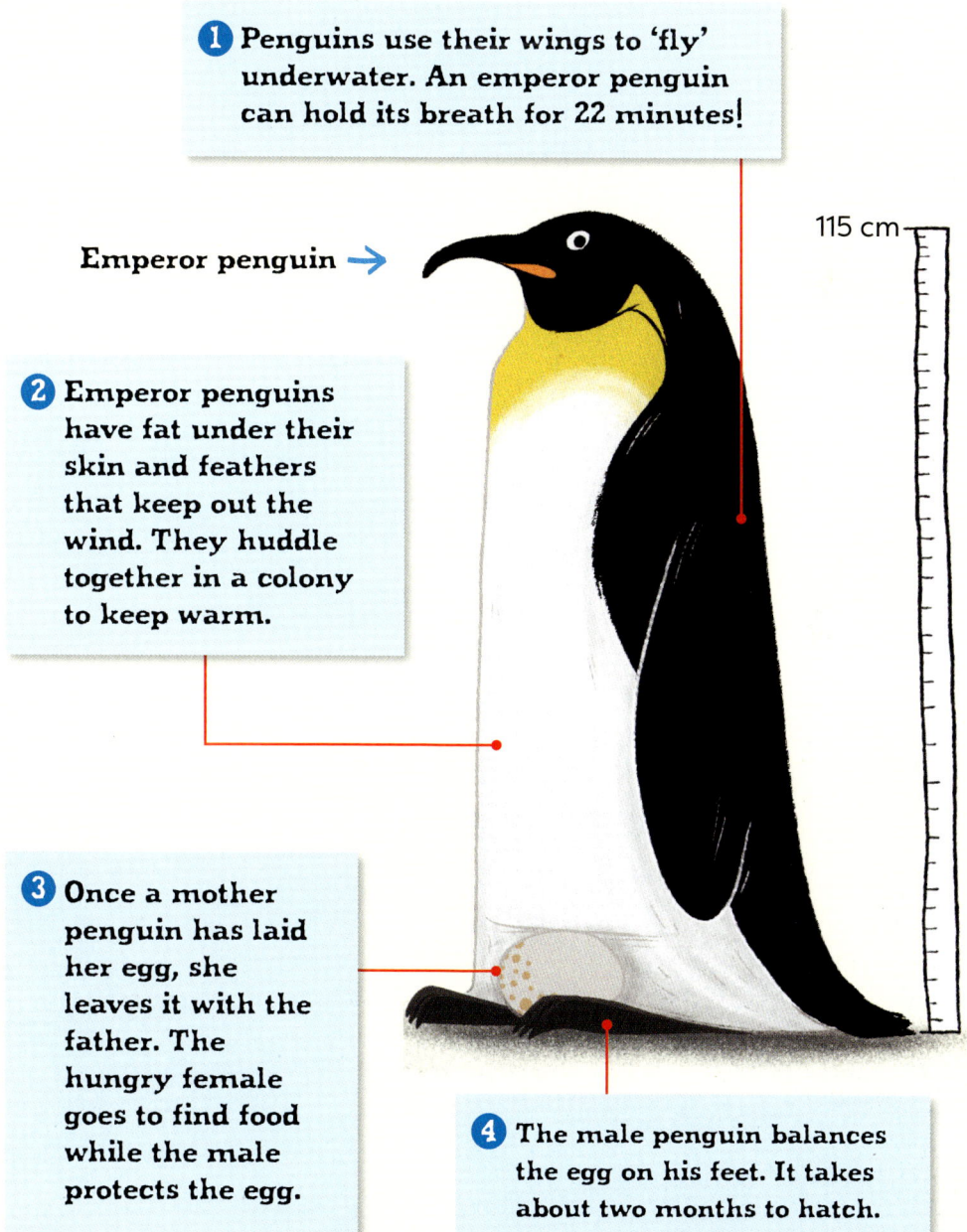

Emperor penguin →

115 cm

1 Penguins use their wings to 'fly' underwater. An emperor penguin can hold its breath for 22 minutes!

2 Emperor penguins have fat under their skin and feathers that keep out the wind. They huddle together in a colony to keep warm.

3 Once a mother penguin has laid her egg, she leaves it with the father. The hungry female goes to find food while the male protects the egg.

4 The male penguin balances the egg on his feet. It takes about two months to hatch.

7 Discovering Endurance

In 2022, a team of scientists formed a mission to the Weddell Sea called Endurance22.

Endurance22

The team wanted to find the location of the long-lost ship, *Endurance*. They were also keen to research **climate change** and the Weddell Sea while looking for the ship.

Others had tried and failed to find *Endurance* beneath the thick slabs of drifting ice. What made Endurance22 different?

Endurance22 was prepared for the wild conditions in Antarctica. Previous expeditions used ships that were unable to withstand the pack ice. Endurance22 used a giant ice-breaker, a ship called *Agulhas II*.

Agulhas II: Key facts

- Built in Finland in 2012, exactly 100 years after *Endurance* was built
- Three times as long as *Endurance*, at 134 metres
- Can break through ice one metre thick
- Has several on-board laboratories for scientific research

← *Agulhas II* breaking through the ice as it makes its way through to the Weddell Sea

Agulhas II was powerful enough to break through the pack ice, and large enough so that the team had a stable base. But how could they see down into the depths of the Weddell Sea? They used a group of special underwater vehicles.

Sabertooth underwater vehicles

Sabertooth robots do not need a human to guide them from inside the vehicle – they are operated by remote control. They also use video and underwater technology to make sure they're in the right place. Sabertooths are small and tough. They are able to travel deep below the surface of the sea without being damaged.

Sabertooths can be controlled from a ship up to 160 kilometres away. This meant that even if the weather was rough, and the ice was too thick for *Agulhas II*, the small, remote vehicles could slip under the surface of the sea and leave the ship and its crew in safer waters.

> **TRUE or FALSE?**
>
> It was much harder to find *Endurance* because Captain Worsley's calculations of the ship's location were wrong by thousands of kilometres. Turn the page to find out!

↓ Worsley's handwritten notes

False! Captain Worsley was an excellent navigator. When *Endurance* sank in 1915, he took lots of measurements using an old type of technology called a sextant. He recorded this information in his diary. As a result, the Endurance22 team knew the area where they should search for the ship.

Sextants

Before computers and modern technology, sextants were used to work out how far north or south a ship was while out at sea. They worked by measuring the angle between the sun and the position of the **horizon**, and comparing this to information written down in special books.

This is how, over 100 years after *Endurance* sank, the famous ship was finally discovered.

Endurance was found, and filmed, by the Endurance22 team on 5th March 2022. The ship sits upright at the bottom of the Weddell Sea, 3000 metres from the surface. It is in amazing condition. You can even see the name *Endurance* on the back of the ship.

The Endurance22 expedition has reached its goal. We have made polar history.

← Dr John Shears, expedition leader of Endurance22

Fact

There are no trees in Antarctica. This is probably why there are no wood-eating creatures in the seas surrounding the frozen continent. In most of the world's seas, a wooden wreck would have been munched up years ago!

A wild white wind sweeps over the land. Emperor penguins shuffle across the pack ice. And down below, in the freezing depths, a famous ship lives a second life. Its smooth wooden beams are home to **filter feeders** such as sea squirts and sea anemones. Sponges hang from its railings like bunting. Brittlestars cling to its **helm**. It's against the law to disturb *Endurance*. The great ship will stay here forever.

The tale of *Endurance* teaches us to never give up. No matter how bad things look, there is always hope. The determination of Shackleton and his crew to survive and escape the ice is part of a real story of endurance.

But it is not the end of the story ...

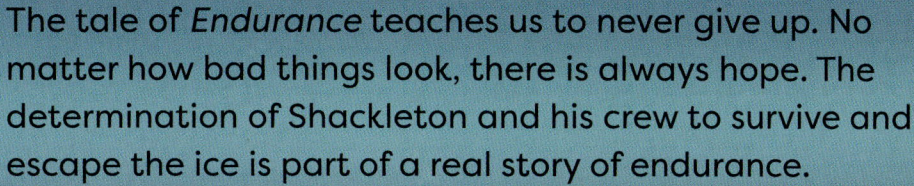

To endure is to continue, against the odds. *Endurance*'s days as a polar explorer ended when it tumbled to the depths of the Weddell Sea. Instead, it has become its own bustling **habitat**. This is, perhaps, the ship's greatest gift. As a base for the wonderful creatures of the Weddell Sea, *Endurance* continues to be part of the circle of life on our beautiful planet.

Glossary

carpenter — a person who builds or repairs wooden things, like houses or ships

climate — the climate of a place is the usual weather you find there

climate change — the long-term change in the temperature and weather patterns of the planet

clockwise — when something is moving clockwise, it is moving in a circle in the same direction as the hands on a clock

continent — a large area of land made up of countries, like Africa or Europe

craft — a vehicle that moves, like a ship or an aeroplane

dock — when a ship reaches land and is brought into harbour

filter feeders — animals that eat by filtering small creatures or bits of food from the water

frostbite — a sickness where parts of the body are badly hurt because of cold, such as fingers and toes

glaciers — giant chunks of ice that move very, very slowly

habitat — the home of an animal, fungus or plant

helm — the part of a boat or ship that is used to steer it

horizon — the line where the Earth and the sky seem to meet

ice-breaker — a large ship that sails through frozen water, breaking the ice as it goes

ice shelf — a mass of ice that is attached to land but floats over the sea

navigate — to plan, manage and control the journey of a ship or aircraft

orcas — large marine mammals that live and hunt in groups

species — a type of plant, animal or fungus whose members can reproduce

stowaway — a person who hides on a ship, aeroplane or train, often so they don't have to pay for a ticket

whaling station — a base for whale hunting

Index

Agulhas II 39, 40, 41

Amundsen, Roald (explorer) 5

Blackborow, Perce (stowaway) 11, 12, 13

breakfast 17

climate 37

climate change 38

commemorative stamps and postcards 33

Discovery 4

Elephant Island 14, 23, 24, 25, 26, 27, 30, 31, 32

elephant seals 30

Endurance22 38–43

expedition plan 10

freshwater 15

frostbite 25

glaciers 15, 27

Hurley, Frank (photographer) 15

ice shelves 15

icebergs 14, 15, 16

ice-breakers 31, 39

James Caird lifeboat 26, 27, 28

lifeboats 21, 22, 23, 24, 25, 30, 32

McNeish, Henry (carpenter) 20, 22, 26, 31

Midwinter's Day 19

Mrs Chippy (cat) 12, 13, 22

Nimrod 4

orcas 23

pack ice 14, 16, 17, 18, 19, 21, 22, 23, 36, 39, 40, 44

penguins 26, 35, 37

polar bears, 26, 27

Polaris 8

Sabertooth underwater vehicles 40, 41

Scott, Captain Robert (explorer) 4, 5

sextants 42

Shackleton family motto 7

Shackleton, Emily 6, 7, 33

sledge dogs 10, 11, 19, 22

South Georgia Island 12, 13, 14, 17, 21, 23, 25, 26, 27, 28, 29, 30, 32

Stancomb-Wills, Janet 7

Terra Nova 5

Weddell Sea 2, 5, 10, 14, 16, 20, 34, 35, 36, 38, 39, 40, 43, 45

whales 35

whaling station 25, 27, 28, 29, 30

Worsley, Frank (captain) 9, 20, 26, 28, 30, 41, 42

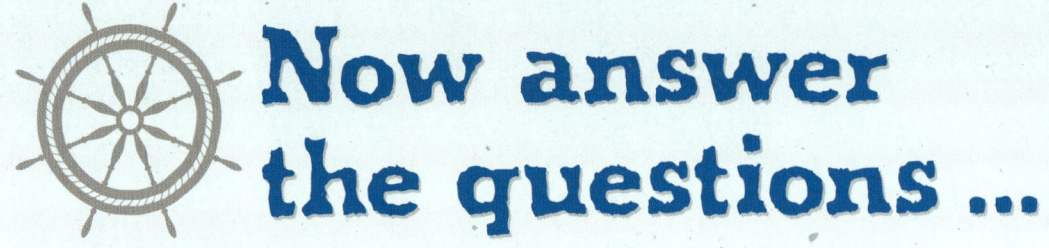

Now answer the questions ...

1. 'Shackleton was raising money for his expedition'. Think of another word that could be used instead of 'expedition' in this sentence.

2. Where and when was Shackleton born?

3. Find a word on page 12 that tells us the author thinks Perce Blackborow was very bold and adventurous.

4. Why were icebergs a danger to *Endurance*?

5. What is the main point in the text on page 18?

6. Why did the author choose to include images of Shackleton before the trip and after he returned to South Georgia Island?

7. What does 'vast' mean on page 36?

8. How are Sabertooth robots operated?

9. Why is it important that *Endurance* is left at the bottom of the Weddell Sea?

10. Do you think Shackleton's mission was a success or a failure? Why?